Awesome Space

THE
UNIVERSE

John Farndon

COPPER BEECH BOOKS
Brookfield, Connecticut

© Aladdin Books Ltd 2001

Produced by:
Aladdin Books Ltd
28 Percy Street
London W1P 0LD

ISBN 0-7613-2251-5

*First published in the
United States in 2001 by:*
Copper Beech Books,
an imprint of
The Millbrook Press
2 Old New Milford Road
Brookfield,
Connecticut 06804

Editor:
Liz White

Designer:
Simon Morse

Illustrators:
Ian Thompson
Graham White
Simon Tegg
Cartoons: Jo Moore

Certain illustrations have
appeared in earlier
books created by
Aladdin Books.

Contents

Introduction

When you look up into the dark sky at night, have you ever wondered what is out there? You may know that the Earth is part of the Solar System, but what is beyond that?

This book will take you off into the far reaches of the Universe. Find out how new planets are formed, discover how gravity works, and learn about the Big Bang that started it all and the Big Crunch that may end it all!

Spot and count!

Q: Why watch for these boxes?

A: They give answers to the space questions you always wanted to ask.

zoom in on...

Space bits

Look for these boxes to take a closer look at space features.

Awesome facts

Look for these diamonds to learn more about the truly weird and wonderful facts about space and the Universe in which we live.

• In this book, a billion is one thousand million.

The Universe

The Universe is very, very, very big—bigger than anything you can possibly imagine. It is not just all the stars, planets, and galaxies, but all the empty space in between as well. In fact, the Universe is everything that exists, from the tiniest bit of an atom to entire galaxies.

Which planet is named after the Roman goddess of love?

Pluto

Uranus

Neptune

Saturn

Jupiter

Mars

Earth

Venus

Sun

Mercury

Q: How big is our Solar System?

A: Our Solar System is so large it would take you over 5,000 years driving in a fast car to get to Pluto, the farthest planet from Earth!

No one knows just how big the Universe is, or even whether it has a definite edge. Some astronomers think it goes on forever. Others believe it is shaped like a donut. But with powerful telescopes scientists can see incredibly bright objects called quasars, which they believe may be on the edge of the Universe. These could be as far as 7 billion, trillion miles away.

Awesome factS
Our galaxy, the Milky Way, seems huge, but the Universe contains at least 100 billion galaxies like ours!

The Big Bang

Scientists have worked out that the Universe began with an enormous explosion. One moment there was nothing, the next, there was a tiny, unbelievably hot, dense ball containing all the matter in the Universe. Then a moment later, the Universe existed, blasting itself into life with the biggest explosion of all time—the Big Bang.

①

②

Q: How do we know about the Big Bang?

A: Every galaxy in the Universe is zooming away from ours. This shows the Universe is expanding. By plotting from the past how it has expanded, astronomers have worked out that the Universe began about 13 billion years ago.

1. No one knows quite why it all started. But scientists think it all began with a small, incredibly hot ball. In the first split second, it grew to the size of a football and then cooled down rapidly.

2. Gravity behaved very strangely. Instead of pulling things together, it blew them apart, and the Universe expanded at terrific speed. In a split second, it grew bigger than a galaxy.

⑤

④

③

3. As the Universe expanded, it cooled, and tiny particles of energy and matter began to appear. These particles formed a dense, immensely thick soup.

4. After about 3 minutes, gravity began to behave as it does now, drawing things together. Particles joined to make atoms, atoms joined to make gases such as hydrogen and helium.

5. Gases clumped into clouds. After several hundred million years, these clouds began to form stars and galaxies. These galaxies merged into clusters and superclusters, and much later the Sun and Solar System were formed. The Universe is still expanding and new planets and stars are still being formed.

Gravity

Every bit of matter in the Universe is pulled toward every other bit by an invisible force called gravity. It is what keeps you on the ground and holds the Solar System and the whole Universe together.

Earth's gravity pulls things to the ground—unless, like rockets, they use powerful engines to push in the opposite direction. Gravity also pulls the Moon into orbit around the Earth.

Exploring rocket

Jupiter is huge and is, in some ways, more like a star than a planet. Made mainly of hydrogen and helium, like the Sun, its strong gravity squeezes these gases until they are hot.

Rocket carrying satellite into orbit.

Jet

The Sun's gravity keeps Earth in orbit around it.

Sun

Gravity is a mutual attraction between every bit of matter. A skydiver has a gravity that pulls, and he falls because he and the Earth pull each other together. But he falls to the Earth rather than Earth falling to him because the Earth is so much heavier and pulls so strongly.

Moon's orbit

Satellite's orbit

Earth's orbit

Q: How is gravity used to find out the size of stars?

A: The pull of gravity between two things like planets or stars depends on how massive they are, and how far apart they are. Astronomers can often tell how big a star is from how strongly its gravity appears to pull on nearby stars or planets.

9

Stars

Stars are the basic units of the Universe. There are nine planets in the Solar System that orbit our star, the Sun. However, astronomers have found at least 50 other planets in the Universe that circle other stars.

Awesome facts

There is a planet circling the distant star 51 Pegasi. Temperatures there are probably a scorching 2,400°F, and a year lasts just 4 days.

1

zoom in on...

New worlds

Even when they cannot see a new planet directly, astronomers may see a disk of matter around a star in which new planets are forming.

Distant stars may have planets circling them that are too small to see, even with a powerful telescope. But as a planet circles a star, its gravity pulls the star slightly to and fro. Astronomers notice that the star's light turns a little redder when the planet is pulling the star away from Earth. It turns bluer when the planet pulls the star toward Earth.

Star

Telescope on Earth

Planet's orbit

Astronomers think planets form from vast disks of gas and dust that spin around certain stars (1). Gravity makes the disks clump together in places to form new planets (2).

2

Awesome facts

The nearest star, Alpha Centauri, is 4.2 light years away from Earth. This means that light would take 4.2 years to travel from this star to Earth.

Astronomers can tell from a star's color how fast it is moving. As it zooms away, the light waves get stretched out behind it. Stretched light waves look redder. The faster it is moving, the more the waves are stretched and the redder it looks.

The growing Universe

The Universe is incredibly big, and it is getting bigger! We know this because every star we can see is rushing away from us. The farther away a star is, the faster it is whizzing away.

To see why galaxies move farther apart as the Universe expands, try this with a balloon. Stick paper stars on a partly inflated balloon to represent the galaxies. Then blow up the balloon more. You can see the stars (galaxies) moving farther apart as the balloon gets bigger.

Light and radiation

All the time, every second of the day and night, stars are beaming energy called radiation at us here on Earth. Some of this radiation, called visible light, is the light we can see. Most radiation, though, is invisible, coming in waves that our eyes cannot detect.

Our eyes can see only visible light. But astronomers have built special telescopes that pick up invisible radiation such as X-rays and radio waves. This means we can see much more of the stars and galaxies than our eyes alone show us. Indeed, stars such as Scorpius X-1 and Cygnus X-1 are known mainly by their X-ray and radio signals.

How light travels

We know that light and other kinds of radiation travel in a straight line, faster than anything else in the Universe. But scientists were long unsure whether light moved like waves in the sea or like a bouncing ball. They now believe it is a combination of both—minute packets of vibrating energy called photons.

Awesome facts

Astronomers' telescopes can register light sent out by distant stars billions of years ago. This light can help us discover the history of the Universe.

Star clusters

Stars are not spread evenly across space. Instead, they huddle together in clumps called clusters, attracted by their own mutual gravity. New clusters are forming all the time, but some are billions of years old.

With the Hubble Space Telescope, astronomers found that clusters contain more stars than were visible before. Hubble showed that this cluster, NGC 1850 (right), thought to contain only about 1,000 stars, actually contains at least 10,000 stars.

What is the other name for the Pleiades?

16

Pleiades

The newest clusters are called open clusters and contain several hundred stars. The Pleiades open cluster in the constellation of Taurus is one of the few clusters in which some individual stars can be seen with the naked eye. However, it also contains hundreds too faint for you to see.

Globular clusters

Around the edge of galaxies, there are about 140 large, old clusters called globular clusters (left). There are often 100,000 stars in a globular cluster, and sometimes up to a million. As the galaxy spins around, so do these clusters, taking about 100 million years to go around the galaxy once.

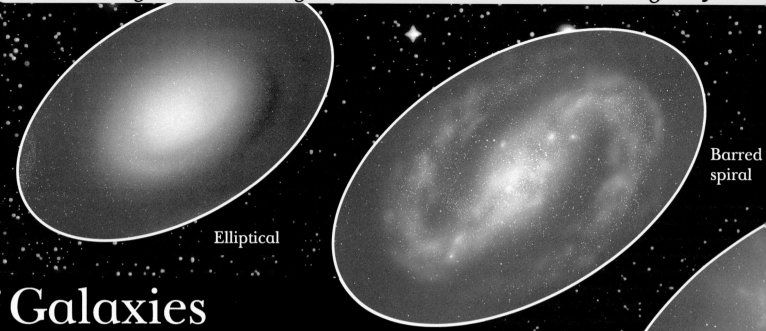

Elliptical

Barred spiral

Galaxies

Just as stars are gathered in clusters, so clusters of stars are clumped into vast star cities called galaxies. The biggest galaxies are incredibly large and can contain thousands of billions of stars.

Galaxies zoom around in all directions. Every now and then they crash into each other. Irregular galaxies like the Small Magellanic Cloud may be the debris from such a galactic pileup.

Q: How old are galaxies?

A: Scientists cannot agree how old galaxies are. Most believe that many elliptical galaxies date back almost to the dawn of time and are at least ten billion years old!

Most galaxies are spiral in shape. A quarter of all galaxies are "irregular." Some galaxies are barred spirals. The biggest galaxies are round or fried-egg-shaped "elliptical" galaxies.

Irregular

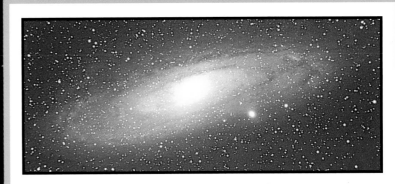

The Andromeda galaxy is the nearest to the Milky Way. It is still so far away that without a telescope it looks just like a faint blur. Two million light years away, it is the farthest thing we can see with the naked eye.

Spiral

The Milky Way

Our Sun is just one of 100 billion stars grouped together in a galaxy called the Milky Way. The Milky Way is often called the Galaxy, but is actually just one of more than 30 billion spiral galaxies in the Universe.

Spot the group of stars represented by a dog.

Canis Major

Puppis

Vela

Carina

Centaurus

Crux

Muca

Triangulum Australe

Ara

Our Sun, with its Solar System of planets, is just one of millions of stars on one of the arms of the Milky Way. The whole galaxy sweeps the Sun around at nearly 62 million mph! The Sun goes once around the galaxy in just 225 million years.

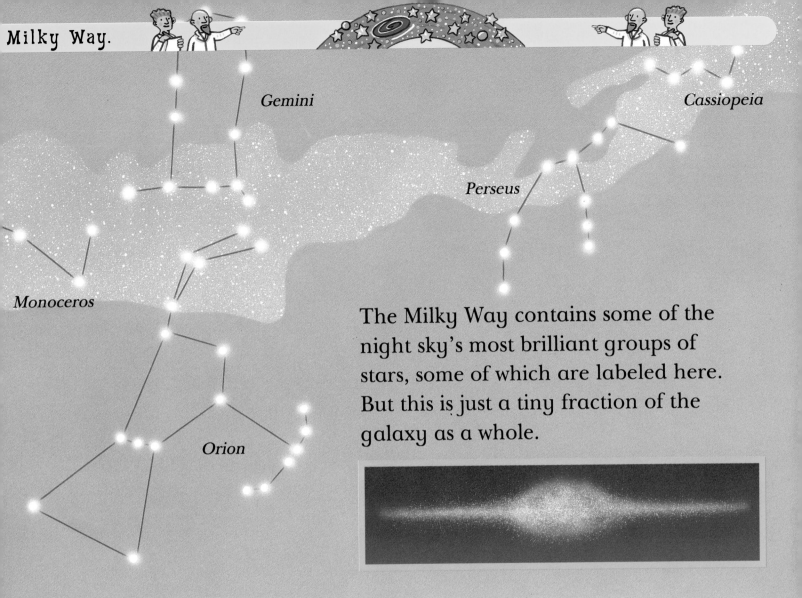

Gemini

Cassiopeia

Perseus

Monoceros

Orion

The Milky Way contains some of the night sky's most brilliant groups of stars, some of which are labeled here. But this is just a tiny fraction of the galaxy as a whole.

Q: Why is it called the Milky Way?

A: If you're far from town on a dark, clear night, you can see a hazy band of light stretching across the sky. You are actually seeing an edge-on view of the Milky Way galaxy with its countless stars. People long ago called it the Milky Way because it looked like someone had spilled milk across the sky.

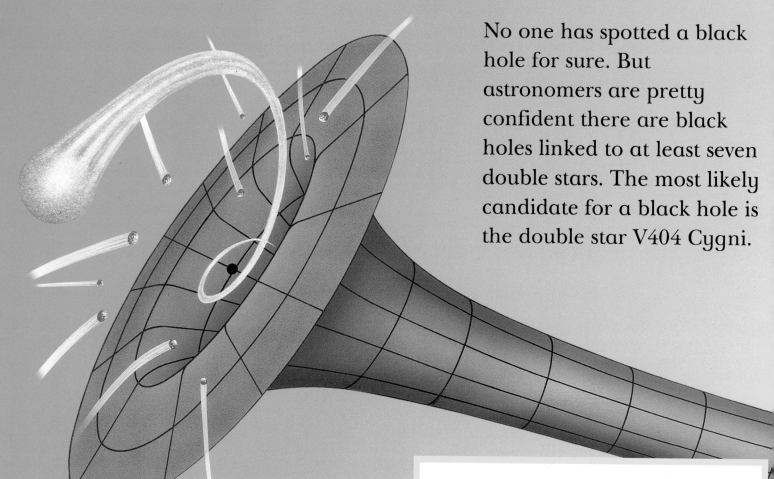

No one has spotted a black hole for sure. But astronomers are pretty confident there are black holes linked to at least seven double stars. The most likely candidate for a black hole is the double star V404 Cygni.

This picture shows a black hole as a funnel because matter, radiation, and even space and time are sucked into a black hole like water down a drain. In fact, a black hole is small and round, and its surface is called an event horizon. If you go beyond the event horizon, you go out of space and time into nothingness.

Enormous black holes may be at the heart of every galaxy, including the Milky Way. These black holes may contain as much matter as millions of Suns, in a space no bigger than the Solar System.

Black holes

Black holes are points in space where gravity is so strong that it sucks in everything. These points even suck in light, so they can't be seen. This is why they are called "black" holes.

Some scientists think there are white holes, too. If black holes are like drains sucking in everything, then white holes are fountains, where it all gushes out again. If we could join a black hole to a white hole, perhaps we could create a tunnel, a short cut, through space.

Some black holes probably form when a huge star burns out. It is squeezed so tightly by its own gravity that all of its matter is crushed into a tiny point before it vanishes completely.

Black hole

White hole

Black hole and white hole separate

Black hole and white hole join, forming tunnel

Active galaxies

We see many galaxies because they beam out visible light. But there are some that beam out powerful surges of X-rays, radio waves, and other invisible forms of radiation. Astronomers call these galaxies active galaxies.

When astronomers look at the galaxy Centaurus-A using X-rays, they see a band of bright spots on either side of the galaxy's core. They believe these bright spots are gas particles, shot out of the core of a black hole, surging through the galaxy's magnetic field.

The jets sent out by the black hole at the core of the Centaurus-A galaxy generate X-rays and radio waves. They beam out radio signals that make the most powerful radio beacon on Earth seem very weak by comparison. The gas jets are 100 times larger than our entire galaxy.

An active galaxy beams out awesome amounts of energy. Astronomers think the source of all this power is a massive black hole that is sucking in entire stars. As the black hole shreds a star, it spews out jets of gas that generate X-rays and radio waves.

A photo of the galaxy Centaurus-A (above) shows a different view from the X-ray photo (left). The galaxy's core is believed to be a massive disk of gas spinning around a huge black hole.

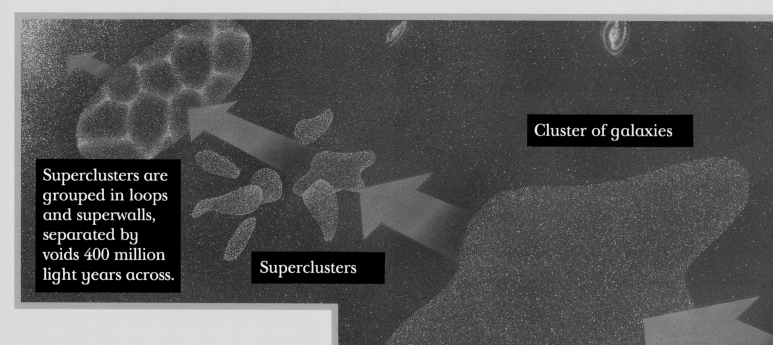

Superclusters are grouped in loops and superwalls, separated by voids 400 million light years across.

Superclusters

Cluster of galaxies

Super-structures

Just as clusters of stars form galaxies, so galaxies group to form even larger structures. Our Milky Way galaxy is over 100,000 light years across, but it is just part of a group of 40 galaxies called the Local Group.

Just as galaxies form the Local Group, so the Local Group is clumped with other groups of galaxies to form clusters of thousands of galaxies. Half a dozen or so clusters are, in turn, grouped into large superclusters 200 million light years across.

Great Wall

The biggest known structure in the Universe is the Great Wall. It is a superwall, a group of superclusters, some 500 million light years across. But even this may not be the biggest structure. There may even be structures three billion light years across!

Local group

Great Wall of galaxies

Milky Way

The Big Crunch

Scientists are looking into the sky for clues about the fate of the Universe. Will it go on growing forever—the open Universe? Will it stop growing and just stay the same size—steady state? Or will it eventually shrink again—the Big Crunch?

Big Bang

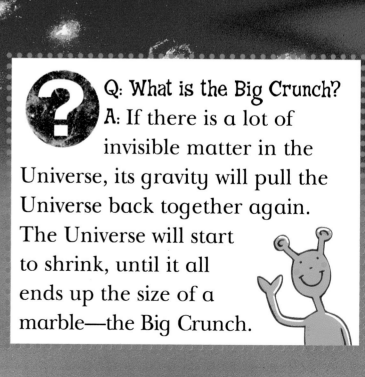

Q: What is the Big Crunch?
A: If there is a lot of invisible matter in the Universe, its gravity will pull the Universe back together again. The Universe will start to shrink, until it all ends up the size of a marble—the Big Crunch.

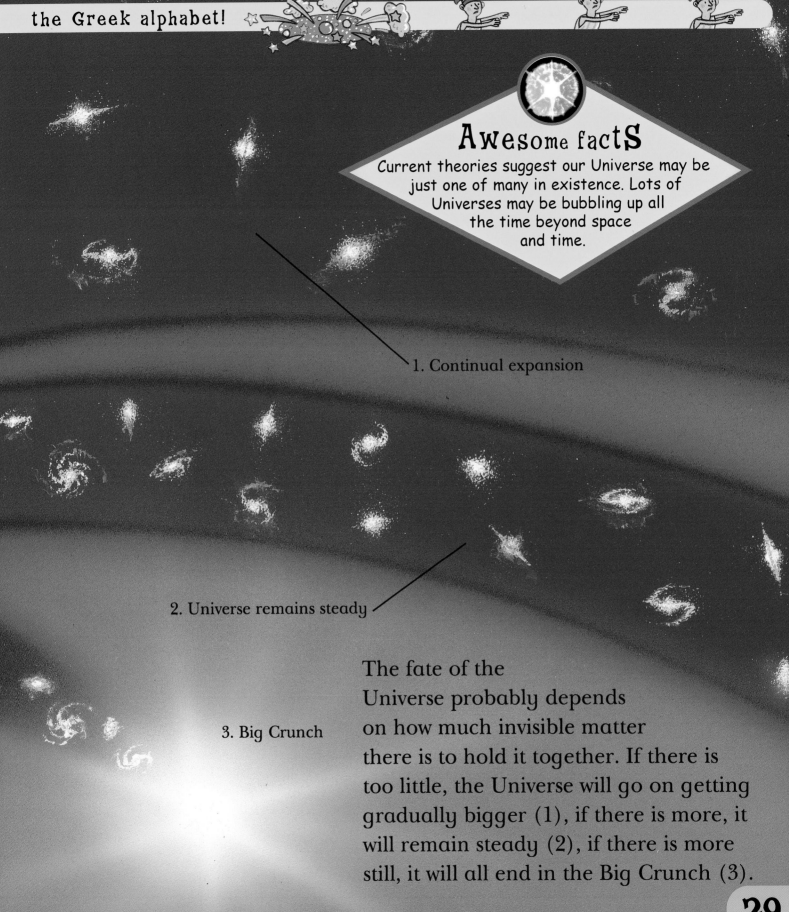

Awesome factS

Current theories suggest our Universe may be just one of many in existence. Lots of Universes may be bubbling up all the time beyond space and time.

1. Continual expansion

2. Universe remains steady

3. Big Crunch

The fate of the Universe probably depends on how much invisible matter there is to hold it together. If there is too little, the Universe will go on getting gradually bigger (1), if there is more, it will remain steady (2), if there is more still, it will all end in the Big Crunch (3).

29

Universe facts

The Universe is enormous and it can be difficult to understand its size. Below is a chart that will give you some idea of the proportions of the Universe!

Milky Way
100,000 light years across

Our Solar System
13 light hours across

Andromeda
our nearest galaxy,
2 million light years
from Earth

Earth

Moon
1 light second
from Earth

Sun
our star,
8 light minutes
from Earth

Pluto
the farthest planet,
5.5 light hours
from Earth

Alpha Centauri
our nearest
star system,
4.2 light years
from Earth

Glossary

Active galaxy

A galaxy that emits huge amounts of radiation, including radio waves and X-rays. Astronomers believe that active galaxies have a black hole at their center.

Big Bang

A huge explosion about 13 billion years ago that many astronomers believe started the Universe.

Big Crunch

A possible end to the Universe. This could occur if all the matter in the Universe is pulled together by gravity, ending in a Big Crunch.

Black hole

The remains of a huge star that has exploded and collapsed in on itself. The gravity is so strong that not even light can escape.

Constellation

A group of stars in the night sky. Astronomers recognize 88 of them.

Galaxy

An enormous cluster of stars. Each galaxy can contain many billions of stars. Galaxies can be spiral, barred spiral, elliptical, or irregular. Our galaxy, the Milky Way, is spiral.

Gravity

A force that attracts every object in the Universe to every other object. The Solar System is held together mainly by the Sun's gravitational pull.

Light year

A unit used to measure distance in space. A light year is the distance light travels in one year, about 6 trillion (6,000,000,000,000) miles.

Matter

Any material that exists and takes up space.

Photon

A tiny packet of vibrating energy.

Quasar

An object in space that emits an enormous amount of energy. Quasars are thought to be at the center of very distant galaxies.

Radiation

Energy that can be visible light or waves that our eyes cannot see, such as X-rays or radio waves.

Solar System

The group of major planets, including Earth, and minor planets that orbit the Sun.

Universe

Everything that exists, from the tiniest atoms to entire galaxies and beyond.

Void

An empty space or area.

Index

Picture credits
Abbreviations: t-top, m-middle,
b-bottom, r-right, l-left
1bl, 16—STScl/Galaxy Picture Library.
1br, 14, 17tr—Ross Ressmeyer/CORBIS.
9—Alistair Wright; The Military Picture
Library/CORBIS. 10, 14br—NASA. 17ml,
25—CORBIS. 19tr—Michael Stecker/
Galaxy Picture Library. 24—Dr. Eric
Feigelson/Science Photo Library.